D1030885

Letters from Russia
1919

Letters from Russia 1919

P. D. Ouspensky

Routledge & Kegan Paul
London, Henley and Boston

First published in 1978
by Routledge & Kegan Paul Ltd.,
39 Store Street, London WC1E 7DD,
Broadway House, Newtown Road,
Henley-on-Thames, Oxon RG9 1EN and
9 Park Street, Boston, Mass. 02108, USA
Set in 11 on 12pt Baskerville by
Kelly and Wright, Bradford-on-Avon, Wiltshire
Printed and bound in Great Britain by
Whitstable Litho Ltd., Whitstable, Kent.

British Library Cataloguing in Publication Data

Ouspensky, P D

Letters From Russia, 1919
1. Russia – Social conditons – 1917–
2. Russia – Politics and government – 1917
1. Title
309. 1'47 '0841   HN523   78-40679

ISBN 0-7100-0077-4

Contents

Introduction

From 1907 until 1913 Ouspensky wrote fairly regularly for a Russian newspaper, mostly on foreign affairs. At the same time he was working on various books based on the idea that our consciousness is an incomplete state not far removed from sleep, and also that our three-dimensional view of the universe is inadequate and incomplete.

Hoping that answers to some of the questions he had posed might have been found by more ancient civilisations, he made an extensive tour of Egypt, Ceylon and India.

On his return Ouspensky learnt that Russia was at war. For a time impending events did not prevent him from lecturing about his travels to very large audiences in St Petersburg and Moscow. But in 1917 while revolution was spreading through all the Russias, and the Bolsheviks were establishing their reign of terror, Ouspensky was living in various temporary quarters in South Russia, in conditions of great danger and hardship.

Until he managed to reach Turkey in 1920 he and those around him were completely cut off from the outside world, unable to receive or send news even as far as the next town, constantly on the alert to avoid being picked up and murdered by the Bolsheviks.

In 1919 Ouspensky somehow found a way to send a series of articles to the *New Age*, which, under the skilful editorship of A. R. Orage, was the leading literary, artistic and cultural weekly paper published in England. These five articles appeared in six instalments as 'Letters from Russia'. They give a detached but horrific description of the total breakdown of public order, and are reprinted here for the first time.

A remarkable feature of the 'Letters' is that while the revolution was in progress and the Bolshevik regime not fully established, Ouspensky foresaw with unusual clarity the inevitability of the tyranny described by Solzhenitsyn fifty years later.

During the winter of 1919 and the spring of 1920 C. E. Bechhofer (afterwards known as Bechhofer-Roberts) was observing events in Russia as a British correspondent who spoke Russian and had previous experience of the country and people. He had met Ouspensky before 1914, both in Russia and in India; he was a regular contributor to the *New Age* and had himself translated the first of Ouspensky's 'Letters from Russia', written in July 1919. In Bechhofer's book *In Denikin's Russia* the author describes the week or two he spent with Ouspensky and Zaharov above a sort of barn at Rostov-on-the-Don. With its pathos and humour this passage makes a fitting epilogue to Ouspensky's smuggled 'Letters'.

Fairfax Hall

Acknowledgments

The publishers wish to thank Collins Publishers, for kind permission to reproduce an extract, and to copy a map, from *In Denikin's Russia* by C. E. Bechhofer, published by Collins in 1921.

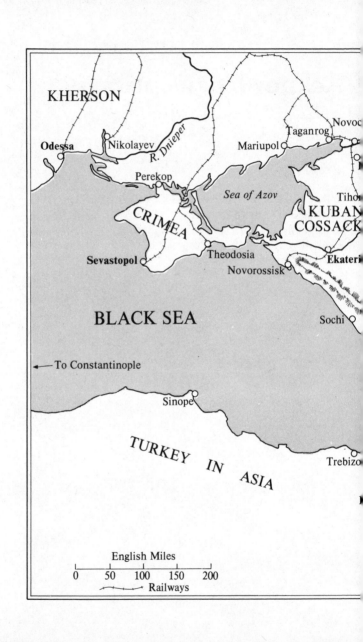

KHERSON

Odessa
Nikolayev
R. Dnieper
Perekop

Taganrog
Mariupol

Novoc

Sea of Azov

CRIMEA

Tiho
KUBAN
COSSACK

Sevastopol
Theodosia
Novorossisk

Ekateri

BLACK SEA

Sochi

← To Constantinople

Sinope

TURKEY IN ASIA

Trebizo

English Miles
0   50   100   150   200
⊢—+—+—⊣ Railways

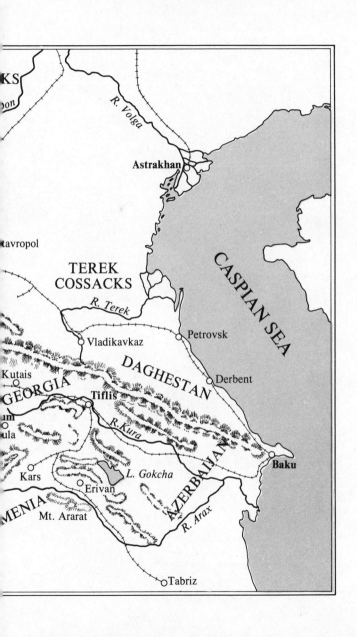

Letter I

Ekaterinodar, July 25, 1919

It is now two years since I last saw the *New Age*, and I do not know what is being said and thought and written in England and what you know. I can only guess. During this period we here have lived through so many marvels that I honestly pity everybody who has not been here, everybody who is living in the old way, everybody who is ignorant of what we now know. You do not even know the significance of the words 'living in the old way'. You have not the necessary perspective; you cannot get away from yourselves and look at yourselves from another point of view. But we did so long ago. To understand what 'living in the old way' means, you would need to be here, in Russia, and to hear people saying, and yourself, too, from time to time, 'Shall we ever live again in the old way? . . .' For you this phrase is written in a quite unintelligible language – do not try to understand it! You will surely begin to think that it is something to do with the re-establishment of the old régime or the oppression of the working classes, and so on. But in actual fact it means something very simple. It means, for example: When shall we be able to buy shoe-leather again, or shaving-soap, or a box of matches?

But, no, it is no use. I feel sure you will not understand me.

You are used to considering questions on a much wider basis; the question of the box of matches will seem to you excessively trivial and uninteresting. I see perfectly clearly that we have lost utterly and for ever the ability to understand one another.

A lady of my acquaintance, whose husband has been abroad all this time, while she has been here with her little son, said to me recently: 'I am frightened of the moment when my husband and I will meet again. He won't understand. Perhaps he will ask me why Alex hasn't been learning English; and I – I shall not know what to say. Indeed, we shall both of us be silent the whole time. Every trifle will create a gulf between us. In the old days we understood one another very well. But now we shall be distant from each other, strangers. . . .'

I understood. We know too much to be able to speak to you on equal terms. We know the true relation of history and words to facts. We know what such words as 'civilisation' and 'culture' mean; we know what 'revolution' means, and 'a Socialist State' and 'winter', and 'bread', and 'stove', and 'soap', and many, many more of the same kind. You have no sort of idea of them.

We know that 'war', and 'politics', and 'economic life' – in a word, all those things about which one reads in the papers, and in which those big two-dimensional creatures called Nations and States live and move and have their being – we know that all this is one thing, but that the life of individual men and women is quite another thing, having no points of contact with the former, except when it does not allow the latter to live. We know now that the whole life of individual men and women is a struggle against these big creatures. We are able to understand without difficulty that a Nation is a creature standing on a far lower stage of development than individual men and women; it is about on the level of the zoophytes, slowly moving in one direction or the other and consuming one another. Thank Heavens we are now beginning to perceive that we are not so.

I am not preparing to set out an esoteric philosophy for your attention. Not in the least. Life, as we see it here, shows us that it is not at all what we used to think it, and that, in any case, we must not regard it as a single whole. A fight is going on within it of blind, struggling forces; and through this fight we are some-how able to steer a course.

If we begin, in what is left of Russia to-day, to examine this life of the great forces, we observe primarily that everything in it acts according to one general rule, which I may call the Law of Opposite Aims and Results. In other words, everything leads to results that are contrary to what people intend to bring about and towards which they strive.

The people who started the war with Germany and pointed out the necessity of destroying Germany and militarism, and so on, did not in the least intend to overthrow the monarchy in Russia and create the Revolution. And the men who dreamed of the Revolution and liberty, and so on, did not in the least expect to bring in the epoch of Kerensky's speeches ('Enough of words; the time is come to act!'). And Kerensky did not intend to create the conditions in which Bolshevism could develop and ripen so well. And the Bolsheviks did not propose to live in a state of perpetual war and to introduce into Russia what is in actual fact the dictatorship of the criminal element. In precisely the same way the

people who are now struggling to bring about the
re-creation of a great, united, indivisible and so on
Russia are gathering results very little resembling what
they are striving for. And, on the other hand, their
opponents – not the Bolsheviks, but those others who
favour the idea of a federation of separate and inde-
pendent States, instead of a single Russia – are destroying every chance of such a division, and are strengthen-
ing the idea of unity.

This side of our own life is very curious and characteristic from the point of view of this same Law. The
idea of self-governing units is in itself very alluring.
The evils of centralisation have long been demonstrated.
But none of the people who used to examine in theory
the status of small self-governing units can ever have
thought that the first coming to life of such organisations would begin with their all fighting with one
another. But this is what happens. Before anything
else is even thought of, the frontiers are closed, customs-
houses are established, passage through their territories
is made difficult, as is likewise the taking in or out of
articles, and then the local politicians start making
speeches about the wicked schemes and general
depravity of the neighbouring State, about the necessity
of getting rid of its evil influence upon local conditions,
etc., etc. And at once the dull rattling of weapons
begins in one direction or the other.

The Russia of to-day presents an interesting picture.
To travel from Mineralny Vody to Rostov and thence
to Novorossisk, you pass through four States, each
with different laws, different prices, different sorts of
police, united only by a single common quality, namely,
that without bribes (and such enormous bribes as were
never even dreamed of in the old Russia) you cannot

go far. For example, for a railway ticket that costs 100 roubles, you have to pay a bribe of 200 or 300, or even 500 roubles. Of course, this is not the case always or everywhere; but, wherever there are any prohibitions, bribes are essential. If you want something more important than a railway ticket, you have to pay correspondingly more. Everyone knows about it. Everyone talks about it. And everyone accepts it as permissible and inevitable. We have understood that it is a point of contact between historical events and the life of individual men and women.

If you want to see what Russia now is really like, try to imagine the following happening in England, then you will see how much more interesting and varied our life is than yours.

The scene is Rostov station about a month ago. The night train for Ekaterinodar is about to leave. There are no tickets to be had. This means that you must pay a porter 140 or more roubles for a third-class ticket costing 40 roubles. For this you get a ticket for a numbered seat. But when the passengers get into the train it appears that for every seat four tickets have been sold. Then even we begin to be irritated. An official appears, something like an old-time gendarme, and invites anyone who wishes, to remain behind and make a complaint. When he is given the number of the porters who sold the tickets, and is told to fetch the stationmaster and the booking-clerk, he merely smiles at the naïveté of the questions and says that these gentlemen are busy.

And now if we turn to the life of individuals and see how it develops 'points of contact' with history, we observe that the pre-eminent subject of conversation is the strangeness of our all being alive (not all, of course,

5

but we who survive), and the reflection that we may all perhaps be alive for a little while longer. The next favourite topic is the high price of everything, generally how much such and such a thing costs.

The prices of all products and necessities have risen by twenty, fifty, a hundred, or six hundred times. Workmen's wages have risen twenty, fifty, or even a hundred times. But the salary of an ordinary 'brain-worker' – a teacher, journalist or doctor – has risen in the best cases by no more than three times, and very often has not risen at all, but has actually decreased. If you earn 2,000 roubles a month, you are considered to be doing well; but often one meets with earnings of 1,000, 800 or 600 roubles. But the cheapest pair of boots cost 900 roubles, a pound of tea 150 roubles, a bottle of wine 60 roubles, and so on. On the whole, you may reckon a rouble now as worth a pre-war kopeck, i.e., its hundredth part.

You will ask how it is possible to live under such conditions. And this is the most occult aspect of the whole question.

I will answer for myself: I personally am still alive only because my boots and trousers and other articles of clothing – all 'old campaigners' – are still holding together. When they end their existence, I shall evidently end mine.

In general, to realise these prices, you must imagine that everything in England has grown correspondingly dear, viz., boots, £90; a suit, £400; a pound of sugar, £10; and that your income remains precisely what it was before. Then you will understand our Russian life to-day.

You must understand, too, the psychological side of these prices. In some people they create panic, in others complete prostration, in others again a kind of mystic fatalism. In primitive people they evoke a thirst for profits, because never in any place were profits made so simply and easily as now in Russia. The prices are different in every place. To carry something from one town to another is to make money. Prices rise by leaps and bounds. At Ekaterinodar, which is considered the cheapest place in Russia to-day, the price of bread doubled itself in a fortnight, rising from $1\frac{1}{2}$ roubles a pound to 3 and even $3\frac{1}{2}$. Everybody realises that this is the result of some big 'deal'. Someone is putting millions into his pocket. But since it is not exactly clear who, in this particular case, is doing it, everybody prefers to be silent. But 'the masses' rush to take part in the general looting, the fascination of which excites their imagination. For a bag of flour or of bread, a basket of eggs, or a jar of butter may bring them a whole fortune as reckoned in the old values. So the trains and stations are crowded with people with bags and baskets; they carry typhus and cholera, and regulate commercial relations between the States of the Don, Terek and Kuban.

This 'speculation' is one of the most prominent symptoms of our life. It began in the first year of the war, and has grown to such an extent that we cannot exist without it. When a 'war upon speculation' is declared, we all begin to groan and cry out. For it means that some article of necessity – milk, butter or eggs – will temporarily disappear altogether from the market, and when afterwards it comes back it will cost three or four times what it cost before.

In nothing has the Law of Opposite Aims and Results appeared more clearly than in the war on profiteering. Nothing seems to touch an ordinary inhabitant who does not take part in speculation so seriously as the war with it.

You will ask what else we live for. Russia was once famous for its literature and its art. Yes, but that all disappeared long ago. Literature, art and science have all been abolished by the Bolsheviks, and they remain abolished.

Ah, but I forgot! The Bolsheviks, I said. I quite forgot that you do not know what this word means. Even if you have seen Bolsheviks in England, believe me they are not the real thing. In my next letter I hope to tell you what Bolsheviks are.

Translated by C. E. Bechhofer

Letter II

Ekaterinodar, September 18, 1919

I recently succeeded in obtaining several copies of English newspapers for the months of July and August. They were the first to come into my hands after more than two years spent in a country completely cut off from the rest of Europe. And I read the old copies of *The Times*, the Newcastle paper, the *North Mail*, as they can only be read by a man who has just been released from gaol or who has returned from a journey to the North Pole. Very soon, however, the first feeling of happiness gave way to another, of fear.

Your people do not see or know anything, just as two years ago we did not see or know anything ourselves. And I wished I could shout to you: 'Look at us, look at our present state! Then you will understand the meaning of what is happening to you, of what is awaiting you if you fail to see in time where you are being led.' All I read in your Press I mentally divided into three groups. The first consists of the usual news-items: latest news, daily events, murders, suicides, the flight of the R.37, the Ulster question, the Prohibition campaign, etc., etc. Behind this news, however, one feels the desire to make everybody believe that nothing exceptional is happening or has happened, and that life continues as before in the customary and well-known way, a little too pronounced to be quite natural.

9

Unhappily in reality this life is already at an end, not in our country alone. Something new, yet unknown, is abroad in your country as well. If you only knew our history for the last two years you would realise what is happening to you and have a look at the future.

The second group of news makes me sure of the fact of the approaching future. I can feel in the letters, articles, etc., a pronounced feeling of fear. The chief topic at present is the high cost of living. You begin to feel the neighbourhood of the precipice! There is, for instance, a letter by Sir Arthur Conan Doyle to *The Times* about the causes of high prices and the means to combat them, or else I find under discussion the Profiteering Bill, and generally everything that is being written and said about prices of coal, dresses, fruits, butter – in fact of everything. Something is happening, and nobody can understand what it really is. All that is being said on the Profiteering Bill is very characteristic. Everybody understands it to be a measure of self-deception, but nobody can think of anything better. And suddenly I fancied daybreak in London, the town yet asleep, and the old Mr Sherlock Holmes leaving his flat in Baker Street accompanied by his faithful friend, Dr Watson. In his long coat with turned-up collar he is going out to look for the causes of the high cost of living. Yesterday again all prices went up, on cabbages and lettuces, and there are no reasons for it. Poor old Sherlock Holmes, you will never succeed in untying the knot in which England is now entangling herself. There is only one way of doing it. Tell Sir Arthur Conan Doyle to send Sherlock Holmes to Russia! I will show him everything; he will understand everything and he will see everything. The seeds that are only just springing up in England have already revealed their flowers and fruits in Russia. And about the qualities of these fruits and flowers there is no doubt possible. I include in this group what is being written about Russia by her friends, i.e., those who consider it necessary to help Russia, and to help her in her struggle with the unknown. There is also here great uncertainty. To help, yes! Of course help is necessary, but a help not too substantial or strong, but such that there may not be any serious results!

And finally, the third group of what can be found in your newspapers. Here, on the contrary, there are no doubts or uncertainty. This news tells of the indignation of the workmen with the policy of the Government in the case of bourgeois-capitalistic Russia. They ask for the immediate recall of the tanks and the armies out of Russia. They threaten a strike if help is continued to the reactionary forces fighting the young Russian democracy. Even better sounds the advice given to liberated Russia to make peace with the Bolsheviks, to draw a frontier and to live peacefully without disquieting Europe. I would like you to understand how we feel when reading this third group of news. Imagine that robbers have broken into your house. They have got hold of almost the whole house, killed half your family, and are starving the rest to death and shooting down people from time to time. At the moment when you have begun to fight the robbers and succeeded in liberating some of the people, you are advised to make peace with the intruders, to give them half of your house, leave the rest of your family in their power and live peacefully yourself without troubling your neighbours. Or imagine the siege of Delhi. The arm es coming to liberate the town are advised to make peace with the besieging armies and leave them to do what they like with the town. If you clearly realise this picture you will understand the true meaning of the advice and the source whence it comes.

There in 'besieged Delhi' are our friends and relatives. Many of those who are now in the South have left their fathers, mothers, wives and children there. We do not know who is still alive and who is already dead. In any case, there are not many of them left. All news that reaches us from there tells us of some-body's death. It is a long time since we have had any other news. Hunger, cholera, typhus, cold, violence, murder and suicides – this is the life of the North. For over half a year the armies of Yudenitch have been near Petrograd. As early as last winter the papers wrote that as soon as the ice broke it would be possible to buy food, Petrograd would be taken. Everybody who had relatives there waited for the spring to come, counting the days and hoping that those who survived the awful winter would be saved. But the Neva was freed from ice, the summer has passed; it is now autumn, and winter is nearing, but Petrograd is still in the hands of the Bolsheviks; and of those who were alive in the spring only a few are left now. The reason for all this is perhaps that the friends of Bolshevism – friends avowed and secret – have succeeded in assembling such a cloud of lies around it that common-sense and reason, all possibility of understanding, have been completely submerged by it. I am sincerely convinced that, could England realise the true meaning of Bolshevism, neither the weariness with the war nor the dislike of being mixed up in foreign matters, nor the urgent necessity for reforms at home, would have prevented the British people from helping Russia. I am quite sure that a regular crusade would have started in England against Bolshevism could the British nation only realise the meaning of events in Russia, their causes and the goal they are leading us to.

But I would like it to be clearly understood that I do not want to start such a campaign, nor do I ask for help for Russia. First of all, I do not believe that the voice of a single man can have any effect on historical events. Secondly, I am not a politician, but merely an observer. Thirdly, it is already too late! In history events are prepared long before they are made public. The months that have elapsed since the Peace Conference have probably outlined the course of events for many years to come. Now we can only wait and see what will be the result. At present, while I am writing this, a fire is breaking out and spreading over Italy. The reason for this, as well as for many other things that will happen in Europe, lies in the fact that when peace was made no decision was taken about extinguishing the fire in Russia.

Now as to England's relationship with Russia, we must acknowledge that England's help to Russia has been very substantial indeed. Without it the Volunteer Army would not have been able to do anything against the Bolsheviks and would have been crushed. To speak quite plainly, I can now sit here and write solely because England helped us. But the struggle with Bolshevism is far from being at an end, and the results are still unknown. The present position can be summed up as follows:— In European Russia the Volunteer Army is scoring successes. It is possible that soon it will be able to save Moscow. But the Bolsheviks are pressing hard on Koltchak and making their way to Siberia. It is quite possible that, evicted from Europe, they will move into Asia. In this case, if they succeed in reaching the Chinese frontier, the position may be transformed and become very disquieting and dangerous for us, and not for us alone. We have to bear in mind that the armies consisting of Chinese have proved to be the hardest fighters and the most reliable force of the Bolsheviks. We know, too, from trustworthy sources, that these Chinese were recruited for the Bolsheviks in China by German agents. Recently the newspapers have brought the news that these agents are continuing their work of recruiting for the Red Army in China and that the Bolsheviks are expecting large reinforcements of mercenaries, ready to fight anybody and go anywhere. If we try to realise the number of such recruits that China is able to furnish the Bolsheviks with, we shall begin to understand that not only our future, but the future of the whole of Europe, may depend on the course events may take during the next few months. The future of Koltchak may be fateful for Europe. Japan can then save the situation by quickly moving her armies into Siberia and Russia. But I doubt whether she will do it. The government of Koltchak is probably delaying and will continue to delay negotiations with Japan. It is not able to offer a bribe serious enough for the eventual help. Meanwhile every moment is of importance, and no price is too high for assistance on condition that it be given quickly, decisively, and to the end. But apart from the procrastination and the superfluous *amour propre* of the Russians themselves, this assistance can be hampered by the competition of America, who also has designs on Siberian concessions. Or still more can the collision of interests between Japan and America in China, which is now assuming the prospect of an actual conflict, have a disastrous effect on their policy.

Behind these unexpected effects of a *mise en scène* I think I can perceive the hand of an experienced German schemer. Be that as it may, the chronologist of our times may note that in the autumn of 1919 the fate of Europe was in the hands of Japan. What Japan will do we shall learn next year. Certainly this is not the only possible way out. We can still hope that Koltchak will succeed in stopping the Bolshevik advance and later in throwing them out of Siberia; or else that Denikin, after capturing European Russia, will succeed in crushing the Red Army before the latter in its retreat to Asia can avail itself of Chinese support. We are hoping for this; it is our duty to hope for it; nothing else is left for us. But the worst is that even in the event of the success of Koltchak and Denikin against the Bolsheviks it allows the latter a long period for doing irreparable harm to Europe and Asia.

Such is the position at present. Unhappily, you do not realise what will happen if the Bolsheviks should gain a victory over Russia, or even if Bolshevism is allowed to remain for some time as a State, governing immense territories in Eastern Europe and Western Asia. The reason why you do not see the harm done to civilisation by the rule of Bolshevism is undoubtedly the fact that you do not realise its true meaning. You mistake it for what it wishes to be mistaken for. But the essence of Bolshevism lies precisely in what it is not mistaken for. You think Bolshevism a political system that can be discussed, but whose existence cannot be denied. In reality, Bolshevism is not a political system at all. It is something very old, that at different times has borne different names. The Russian language of the eighteenth century knew a name, preserved until now – 'pougachevchina' – which renders very well the essence of Bolshevism. Pougachev was a Ural Cossack who pretended to be the deceased Emperor Peter III, and who raised an insurrection against Catherine II, and for a time succeeded in seizing half of Russia. He plundered the estates of landowners, hanged their owners and priests, gave the land to the peasantry, etc. A classical description of the 'pougachevchina' is to be found in a novel by our poet Pushkin, *A Captain's Daughter*. But Bolshevism of the twentieth century has one peculiarity – it is 'made in Germany', and Germany knows how to make use of it. Employing Bolshevism in 1917 to break up the Russian Army, Germany destroyed the danger menacing her Eastern front. You were in great peril, and you know it. But now you have decided that the peril is gone, and you are mistaken. Germany is not annihilated or even weakened. She is energetically and cleverly preparing a *revanche*. Her chief enemy is England, and the chief trump in her pack is Russian Bolshevism.

Translated by Paul Leon

Letter III

Ekaterinodar, September 25, 1919

In the meantime the state of Russia, even in parts long liberated from the Bolsheviks, remains difficult, and, strange to say, is becoming worse compared with what it was immediately after the Bolsheviks were expelled. Prices rise above all possible count. In the average they are one hundred times, and in many cases two, three, or even many more hundred times, higher than before. I quote several instances to give you a better idea of the position, and give the prices in pounds at the pre-war rate. Ordinary writing paper costs £3.10s. for twenty-seven sheets; a newspaper of small format is sold at 6s. There are no books to be bought. Old schoolbooks are worth almost their weight in gold. A steel pen is bought for 2s. or 3s., tea for £16 to £20, coffee for £6 a pound. Bread in Ekaterinodar, which is supposed to be the cheapest place in Russia to-day, costs 5s. or 6s. a pound. In other places, e.g., Novorossisk, or in the Terek district, it is sold at 10s. to 12s. a pound.

How people manage to live at such a cost is a riddle to me. The pay of the workmen or the small office-holders has increased, if not as much as prices, at least in a certain proportion to them; but the pay of brain-workers has often decreased compared with what it was before the Revolution, and in several instances has disappeared altogether owing to unemployment. And, God knows why, it is considered that a 'brain-worker' has no right to protest or to claim any improvement of his position.

I spent the winter in a small town of the Terek district. There the teachers of public schools (gymnasia) did not receive their salaries, i.e., they got neither the full amount nor did they get it when it was due. For some sort of reason, however, this is considered to be quite natural, and nobody takes any notice of it.

The Government does something for the military and its own immediate workers. But people not engaged in either military or other Government work are left to themselves, deprived of all assistance and of their elementary rights. It sounds like a joke, but it is reality; if you are not on military service you cannot get a railway ticket unless you are prepared to pay an enormous bribe. Many towns are closed to you, nor are you allowed to rent a room or a flat.

'The right to live', i.e., a written certificate authorising you to reside in any particular place – a measure which used to be applied to Jews – is now a rule for everybody. I do not know whom we have to thank for such a brilliant solution of the problem of personal rights, but facts remain facts.

Broadly speaking, the Russia that existed before is gone, and gone long ago. There is a bewildered and hungry country, where people are thrown out of railway carriages; where every conception of cultural values is gone; where any intellectual life ceased long ago; where, at the same time, the number of people under the command of somebody or other is continually increasing. And the sole aim of these persons who command is to improve their own position at the expense of those who are deprived of all rights.

Bolshevism is a poisonous plant; it poisons, even if extirpated or trampled on, the very soil in which it grew, and everybody who gets in touch with it. Perhaps those who fight it are poisoned more strongly by it than anybody else.

If you were to talk with a simple Russian peasant about the essence of Bolshevism, this is probably the plain and open-hearted description you would hear: 'Everything for oneself or those nearest you, and nothing for the others.' Unhappily, this is the most poisonous seed in Bolshevism.

We have come back again to Bolshevism as the cause of everything that happens now in Russia.

Bolshevism begins with loud and fierce declamations. To pave its way it chooses the whole arsenal of extreme socialistic and political doctrines. It promises the people all that they ever dreamt of, all they could dream of. Never for a moment does it think of what can or cannot be fulfilled.

These boundless promises form the outstanding feature of what I call the 'first phase' of Bolshevism.

Hungry, weary, injured, scarcely rational people begin to believe. They always believe when something is promised to them.

The Russian Bolsheviks promised peace. It was their trump card; their struggle against the tragico-comic government of Kerensky in 1917.

The personal staff of the advocates of Bolshevism is also a peculiar thing. It consists in its greater part of neurasthenics. A little note I read in one of the English newspapers told me a lot. The Bolshevik literature was brought over to England by Mrs Pankhurst. There are names that always mean a lot.

The first phase of Bolshevism is composed of words; first of all promises, then calls to vengeance, lies, defamations, and again promises and promises.

People with little culture, and thrown out of the usual course of their lives, are easily and deeply affected by such fireworks of words. They believe and follow those madmen, or scoundrels, who lead them towards the precipice.

The change that occurred in the meaning of the word 'Bolshevik' is also very peculiar. The word itself sounds very awkward and foreign in Russian. It is not a very exact and grammatical translation of the word 'Maximalist'. But the Russian people attached to it a meaning of their own. I personally overheard a conversation two years ago between two soldiers. One of them, who, judging by his appearance, was of very 'advanced ideas' (they used to be called then comrade-deserters), gave a lesson to another, a naïve village boy. 'We are the greater number, do you understand,' he was saying, 'and, therefore, we are called Bolsheviks.'

For him, apparently, the word 'Bolshevik' corresponded to the word 'majority', and this is the sense that is still very widespread among the public.

I overheard this conversation on one of the journeys I had to undertake in the summer of 1917. Several times I had to cross Russia from Petrograd to Trans-caucasia and back again. On the first of these journeys I met with another 'phase of Bolshevism', turning already from words to deeds, and using for its purpose different people and different arguments.

It took us five days to travel from Petrograd to Tiflis, where we arrived in the middle of the night. The railway station was crowded with soldiers – it was the Caucasian Army leaving the front and dispersing under the influence of Bolshevik propaganda. We were told that it was unsafe to walk through the town at night, and we had to wait until the morning. I had hardly slept at all during the journey, and now I was slumbering, sitting in the buffet in an armchair. Suddenly terrifying cries and shouts were heard on the platform, quickly followed by several shots. The company was, of course, panic-stricken; all jumped from their seats, fearing what was to come. Very soon, however, soldiers rushed into the buffet, shouting 'Comrades, do not worry; we have only shot a thief.' It appeared that they had seized somebody who had stolen three roubles out of somebody's pocket, and had therefore shot him on the spot. Over the body of the murdered man a meeting began to gather discussing whether it had been the right thing to do or not. The meeting was so excited that it very nearly came to blows and shots. The clamour was terrifying; several of the passengers went to look at the body of the deceased man lying on the platform.

An hour later there were more shots and cries – another thief was seized and shot. Towards daybreak a third thief was shot, but it appeared that he was not a thief at all, but a militiaman – i.e., a policeman. All this happened on the platform, separated from us merely by a glass door. The general trouble was so great that nobody could understand anything. There on the platform lay three bloodstained bodies.

Of course, this was only the beginning. The soldiers were still friendly towards the public. The time had not yet come; everybody was still getting bread and shoes. But it was quite clear that as soon as there should be no bread and shoes, those with guns would get bread and shoes from those without guns.

While this process of 'deepening' the Revolution was taking place, the leaders of Bolshevism were making their way to power. At last, thanks to murder, lies, unrealisable promises, and using all criminal elements available in Russia, they succeeded in reaching their object. But now they found themselves in a really tragical position. I would like it to be clearly understood how tragic their position was. The Bolsheviks had no constructive programme, and in fact they could not have one. Everybody realised that none of their promises could be fulfilled. They had only to sit quietly and not stir. Any move they made rendered matters worse. It was enough to 'nationalise' a product for it to disappear from the market. 'Socialised' works and factories were busy at meetings and did no work. Life itself taught the Bolsheviks that they had only to continue the revolutionary policy of Kerensky – i.e., to print paper money and make speeches. If they did not like it, it was left to them to fly to Switzerland to arrange conspiracies and start terrorism against Bolshevism in Russia. I think that they themselves realised at that time that they were unable to do anything; the possibility of achieving any creative work was denied to them – their work was destruction alone. They were saved for some time by the struggle that started against them.

But the destruction was at that time an accomplished fact. Russian life no longer existed. All that has happened since is nearer to death than to life. In fact, Russian life was brought to a standstill from the first moment of the Revolution. This moment meant the destruction of any possibility of cultural work. Unhappily, only a few understood its real meaning.

The following is a personal opinion: the public, the

man in the street, had a deeper insight into the Revolution and understood the events much better than the representatives of the Press, the literary men, and especially the politicians. These had lost all power of reasoning and were carried away by the whirlwind of events. Unhappily, their opinion was estimated to be Russian opinion, and, what is worse, they themselves mistook their views for the will of the nation.

It was at that time considered obligatory to profess joy in regard to the Revolution. All who did not feel it had to remain silent. Many, of course, understood that there was nothing to rejoice about, but they were scattered, and even had they spoken their voices would not have been heard in the general chorus of delight.

I well remember one evening of the summer of 1917, in Petrograd. I had been on a late visit at General A.'s, whose wife was a well-known artist, and I was returning home at night with M., the editor of a large artistic monthly. We had to stroll through the whole town. The whole evening through we never mentioned politics. Our host was right in the middle of political life, but he realised plainly enough the hopelessness of all efforts, and politics were in this house felt to be a skeleton at the feast. Only when out in the street did the topic of our conversation become politics.

'Do you know,' said M., 'there are idiots, even among cultured people, who feel happy in the Revolution, who believe it to be a liberation of something. They do not realise that, if it means liberation, it is liberation from the possibility of eating, drinking, working, walking, using tramways, reading books, buying newspapers, and so on.'

'Just so,' I said. 'People don't understand that if anything exists, it does so thanks to inertia. The initial push from the past is still working, but it cannot be renewed! There lies the horror. Sooner or later its energy will be exhausted and all will stop, one thing after another. Tramways, railways, post – all these are working, thanks to inertia alone. But inertia cannot last for ever. You will realise that the fact of our walking here and that nobody is assaulting us is abnormal. It is made possible by inertia alone. The man who very soon will be robbing and murdering on this very spot has not yet realised the fact that he can do it now without fear of punishment. In a few months it won't be possible to walk here at night-time, and some months later it will be unsafe to do it during the day.'

'Undoubtedly,' added M., 'but nobody sees it. All are expecting something good to happen, although nothing was ever so bad before, and there are so few reasons to expect anything good to happen.'

I have never seen M. since that evening, and do not know what has happened to him. Nor do I know if General A. and his wife are still alive, but I have often, in the course of these two years, remembered this conversation. Everything unhappily, has proved the truth of our conclusions so closely.

The next 'phase of Bolshevism' proved to be a touching community with another trait of Russian war life, and very soon this trait became the outstanding feature of Bolshevism. The original cause of the destruction of Russia, what led to the Revolution, was robbery – i.e., what you as a polite and cultured people call profiteering.

Marauding began with the first month of the war and penetrated continuously farther and deeper, sucking out the very spirit of life. No measures were taken against it in Russia, and it grew quickly and immensely and ate up all Russia. Bolshevism, as I have pointed out, assimilated itself to robbery. The masses wanted to have their share in the general plundering of Russia. Bolshevism sanctioned this plundering and gave it the name of Socialism.

I remember a comic occurrence in Petrograd in the same summer of 1917. A strike was called of the employees in manufacturing and haberdashery shops. A crowd of the employees, men and girls, walked in procession along the Nevsky from one shop to another, requiring them to be closed. I was on the Nevsky with a friend of mine. He became interested in the matter and inquired from a young man, obviously very proud of his new role of a 'striker', about the causes and aims of the strike. The lad began hurriedly and excitedly on an explanation.

'They,' he said, 'have profiteered since the beginning of the war. We know very well how much was paid for different articles and at what prices these were sold. You cannot conceive what profits they made.'

'Well,' asked my friend as a joke, 'you undoubtedly require now the reduction of prices and the return of unfairly made profits?'

'No-o,' answered the young man, obviously confused; 'our claims are made according to the programme.'

'What programme?'

'I don't know. In fact, the Party advised us that all salaries are to be raised by 100 per cent (or 60 per cent – I do not remember), and "they" won't give us it. "They" agree to do it from January; they want to save the profits made for the two years past. But we won't leave them alone.'

The question was quite simple. Young men and

25

girls had for three years running witnessed a daylight plundering, and now demanded their share in the robbery. They were led by a party – which party it was I do not even know, but surely it was not the Bolshevist Party. This was busy with other questions. At that time, however, all parties were working for Bolshevism.

Translated by Paul Leon

Letter IV

Ekaterinodar

My friend proved to be a true prophet. Very soon 'sharing in the plunder for the whole time it had been going on' became the leading principle of Bolshevism. Meanwhile – i.e., autumn, 1917 – the actual traits of Bolshevism began to reveal themselves. They form the very essence of the movement, and their application consisted in a struggle against culture, against the 'intelligentsia', against freedom of any kind. People now began to realise the true meaning of Bolshevism; they began to lose the illusions which led them to confuse Bolshevism with a socialistic and revolutionary movement. These illusions, which we have lost, seem now to prevail among yourselves. Persons inclined to abstract modes of thinking persist in seeing in Bolshevism not what it actually is, but what it ought to be according to their theoretical deductions. These people will have a very sad awakening, and this awakening is not 'beyond the mountains', as the Russian proverb says.

The causes of the success of Bolshevism in Russia, which came as a surprise to the Bolsheviks themselves, can be found in the complete destruction of the economical bases of Russian life brought about by the war, in the incredibly mixed political views prevailing among the Russian intelligentsia, varying between patriotic chauvinism and anarchical pacifism, and chiefly in the instability of Russian political thought and the purely theoretical and demagogic character of the chief Russian political parties and tendencies. There was no party created by reality and resulting from actual existing conditions. All that was opposed to Bolshevism consisted of theories alone, theories and phrases very often the same as those employed by the Bolsheviks themselves.

The Bolsheviks knew what they were aiming at; nobody else knew. This is the reason for their success. Of course, their success is only temporary, as, generally speaking, nobody can be a Bolshevik for ever. It is a sickness from which people either recover or, if its germs have entered too deeply into the organism, they die.

Lately the comparison of Bolshevism with disease has become common. This is not sufficiently true. Bolshevism is not only a disease; it is death, and a very quick death, or it is not real Bolshevism.

Bolshevism in general is a catastrophe, a shipwreck.

This is what you do not realise, and you will be able to realise it only when you learn our history of the last three years.

All the political tendencies which existed before the Revolution may be divided into four groups. The first group was the monarchical – i.e., the group that supported the Government. It consisted of people who sympathised with the Government partly on grounds of principle, partly on those of personal interest. Theoretically, they desired a return to autocracy, but actually their wish was only to recover and retain their privileged position. These people did not form a strict political party. The latter was formed by various organisations of nobles and political groups like the 'Union of the Russian People' or the 'Union of Archangel Michael'. Their programmes and tactics were very limited, and consisted chiefly in petitioning for and obtaining from the Government special grants and in the organisation of Jewish pogroms.

The second group was formed by the 'Octobrists'. This party emerged from the Revolution of 1905, and its official aim was the realisation of the principles included in the Emperor's Manifesto of October 17, in which Russia was promised all sorts of freedoms. The actual activity of this group was the struggle against any such realisation. This party was formed by wealthy bourgeois and members of the bureaucracy or of the intelligentsia who liked liberal sentiments without wishing to break away from the Government. A well-known anecdote relates how the Emperor Nicholas II, wishing to be very agreeable to somebody, said: 'I am the first Octobrist in Russia.' The comment made on it was 'that was because he had signed the Manifesto but had not carried it out.'

The third group embraced the so-called 'Cadets', the word being a combination of the first letters of the Constitutional-Democratic Party. Its programme was too theoretic; its origin was to be found in the political clubs gathered round Moscow University. They wanted to remain 'legal', and therefore did not publicly declare their real republican and socialistic tendencies. Its vital element was constituted by the members of the former Zemsky Sojous, who joined the party some time after its constitution. But they were bound by the programme of their party, whose principle had more platform significance than anything else – e.g., universal suffrage on the principle of the direct, secret, and equal ballot.

If the Octobrists were insincere in one way, the

Cadets were in another way, and both were equally different from what they professed to be. They were hampered by the controversial character of several points in their programme and a certain 'party discipline'. Many of its members were highly respectable, esteemed, and energetic men, who formed a group somewhat outside the party proper. They were completely lost among the rank and file of the party, and the mass of the most important members who had actual vital political experience, who knew the country and the people, never played any leading role in the party. The lead was usually taken by theorists of the professional and barrister class. All this deprived the party of strength and actual value. Its left wing was too closely connected with the socialistic parties to be of real vitality and energy.

In the fourth group we can include all the socialistic parties, working on ready-made plans and differing very little from their colleagues abroad. Their division into different groups brought into prominence two chief divergent groups: the 'Social-Revolutionaries' basing themselves chiefly on their 'agrarian policy', and the 'Social-Democrats' – orthodox Marxists. The latter party was itself subdivided into two groups – those who advocated the 'minimum' programme, the Mensheviks, and those advocating the 'maximum' programme – the Bolsheviks. The most vital tendencies in the socialistic parties were the former 'Narodniki', united to a certain extent with the Social-Revolutionaries, or the Narodnyie-Socialists (Socialists of the People), who were of a less extreme tendency. Their success was hampered, however, by the socialistic ballast of their programmes.

The Revolution provoking the fall of the old régime

brought to a natural end the activity of the Monar
chists and Octobrists as political parties. There
remained the 'Cadets', who now openly embraced the
republican faith, and the different kinds of Socialists.
Neither the 'Cadets' nor the Socialists were in a
position to offer effective resistance against the activities
of the Bolsheviks. The different groups of Socialists,
however loudly they protested against the means used
by the Bolsheviks, did not cease to regard them as part
of their own political group. They addressed them as
'comrades' and found it possible to discuss terms of
agreement with them. The attempts to arrive at real
agreements were, of course, doomed to failure, for
every agreement requires a certain amount of honesty
or seriousness from both sides. But Bolsheviks never
considered these agreements with seriousness. The
chief aim of their game was to gain time and their
chief object to obtain power. The rest of the Socialists
did not venture to protest strongly enough or actively
oppose people who repeated their own phrases about
the labour system, about the struggle with capitalism,
and the victory of the proletariat. The 'comrade-
Bolsheviks' only laughed at the sentimentality of the
'comrade-Socialists', and using them as blind tools for
their purposes worked for their aims and achieved what
they wanted.

This was the extraordinary period of a 'comrade-
Premier' and Commander-in-Chief, the barrister
Kerensky. The 'Cadets' tried to save the last remnants
of common sense, but found it impossible to work in
common with the Socialists. The Socialists, on the other
hand, were ready for an agreement with the Bolsheviks.
The road to the victory of Bolshevism lay open.

* * *

Only after two years of humiliation and suffering has Russia succeeded in organising a Centre which does not consider it possible to compromise with Bolshevism. This Centre is for the present at the place where I am now writing, the headquarters of the Volunteer Army.

You surely do not know what this Volunteer Army really is. Its now enormous organisation has developed out of a little detachment of 3,000 men who in February 1918, began their struggle under the leadership of General Kornilov. The legendary expedition of this detachment which came to an end at the death of General Kornilov near Ekaterinodar on March 31, 1918, laid the foundation of the struggle with Bolshevism. It is described in a book written by A. A. Savorine under the title *The Kornilov Expedition*. It is almost the only book published in Russia during the last two years. In a later letter I hope to summarise its contents and to describe the origin of the Volunteer Army, whose history is also the history of the most recent years of Russia.

Even now it would be possible to fill many pages with an analysis of Volunteer activity. In many cases its energies are too much directed towards the restoration of the bad features of the old régime and developing them to a degree worse than they have ever been before. On the other hand, it is in many ways much too tolerant of events which are the heritage of the Provisional Government and the Bolshevik rule.

Only the future can show what is to be the result of all this. At present one thing is of importance. The Volunteer Army is fighting the Bolsheviks and struggling for a united Russia. Accordingly, Russia and the Volunteer Army are now one and the same thing.

Speaking of Russia you speak of the Volunteer Army and vice versa.

But during the first six or nine months of the Revolution no such Centre existed. Russia was then represented by Bolshevism 'made in Germany', united with the 'real Russian' profiteering, and fostered by the absurd idealism of the intelligentsia who quoted the text 'Do not overcome evil by evil.' In face of the weakness of the intelligentsia, Bolshevism very soon showed its real face. It began openly to wage war on culture, to destroy all cultural values, and to annihilate the intelligentsia as the representative of culture. The 'Nihilism' of former times was already well acquainted with contempt for culture, as if the only valuable results of the progress of humanity were high explosives. Bolshevism developed this idea to the utmost. Everything that did not help or foster the production of bombs was declared to be valueless, 'bourgeois', and deserving only of destruction and contempt. This point of view was very acceptable to the imagination of the proletarians. The workmen were at once made equals with the intelligentsia, and were even declared superior to it. Everything in which they differed from the intelligentsia was now proclaimed unnecessary and even hostile to the interests of the people and the idea of freedom. The leaders of Bolshevism openly professed that all that they asked of culture was the means of fighting the bourgeoisie and to obtain power for the proletariat. Science, arts, literature, were put under suspicion and were handed over to the watchful control of illiterate bodies of workmen. The newspapers underwent a treatment which the chiefs of the gendarmes of Nicholas I never dreamt of. From the moment the Bolsheviks seized power, all newspapers were shut down. Their place was taken by official or semi-official illiterate Bolshevik *Tsvtias* (News) or *Pravdas* (Truth). In indescribable forms these papers praised the Soviet power and poured out contempt on the 'bourgeoisie'. An unofficial paper (socialistic, of course) was allowed to be printed on condition that it formally supported Bolshevism, – 'recognised the Soviet power' was the official expression. This meant the re-cognition of this power as democratic and the best in the world. It involved also the necessity of expressing the loyalty of the paper by publishing defamations and denouncements of the 'bourgeoisie' and by vile criticism of everything that was not immediately connected with Bolshevism or the Soviets. With the object of preserving the papers from any other kind of influence they were subjected to the control of the workmen of the office where the paper was printed. Their representatives formed the majority of the 'editorial body', which was empowered to dismiss old members of the staff, to appoint new ones, and generally to control the editorial administration. Even the most tolerant and unpretentious journalists had to cease their work, and very soon every journal became the prey of self-seeking people without knowledge of any kind of journalistic work.

Officially the struggle was directed against the 'bourgeoisie'. But this term in its Bolshevik interpreta-tion embraced the whole of the intelligentsia. All persons belonging to the professions, professors, artists, doctors, engineers, and generally all specialists were proclaimed bourgeois indiscriminately and subjected to the control of their own workmen and servants. In a way their position was worse than that of the journalists. The latter were left alone, but doctors, engineers, and civil servants were forced to work under the most incredible conditions. Workmen and guards controlled their engineers; doctors were superseded by councils of patients and porters. This is not a joke – it is real life and obtains at this moment in Soviet Russia. In the spring of 1919, notwithstanding the difficulties created by Bolshevism and the Soviets, the doctors of Soviet Russia assembled in the yearly 'Girogov' meeting held in honour of the late well-known surgeon, Girogov. The evidence collected on that occasion showed that the doctors were quite helpless in combating epidemics owing to the control exercised over them by medical attendants who filled all the responsible offices.

War on the intelligentsia was inevitable on the part of Bolshevism. The intelligentsia could not be deceived for long. It would soon have discovered the underlying lies of Bolshevism. To render the intelligentsia harmless, to prevent its explaining the truth to the people, it was proclaimed bourgeois, its members declared outlaws, and purposely confused with the bourgeois against whom the struggle was originally directed. This was logically inevitable. The intelligentsia, being inclined, generally speaking, to believe in revolutionary phrases, would have otherwise joined Bolshevism and driven it to another line of development. It would have insisted on meeting the debts to which Bolshevism had attached its signature without dreaming of paying anything. In other words, the intelligentsia would have insisted on the fulfilment of the promises given by the Bolsheviks to the people, which the Bolsheviks themselves consider only as a bait thrown to make fishing easier. Had the intelligentsia not been so decidedly denied participation in the Revolution it would have spoiled the game of Bolshevism. The Bolsheviks would never have been able to humiliate Russia to the degree they have. The appropriateness of their measures – i.e., the ostracism of the intelligentsia – is so striking that it involuntarily evokes the thought of a German invention, so well did it fit the purpose of the new Bolshevik state.

As a general rule, Bolshevism based itself on the worst forces underlying Russian life. How far they have succeeded in bringing those forces into existence is a question with which I will deal separately. The provocation of the feelings of the people against the intelligentsia was a thing more easy to achieve in Russia than anywhere else, for the Russian 'people' are as a rule suspicious of every 'gentleman'. In Russia all epidemics of cholera are always connected with rumours of doctors poisoning wells or their patients in the hospitals and are usually followed by pogroms of doctors.

A special aspect of Bolshevism has not yet been sufficiently insisted on. I mean the participation in it of decidedly criminal elements. In former days the population of Russian prisons used to be divided into two classes, the minority of 'comrade-politicals' and the vast majority of 'comrade-criminals'. I think that nobody of the 'comrade-political' ever dreamt that the leading part in the Revolution would be played by the 'comrade-criminals'. But this is the truth. The future historian will have to think out a new definition for the Soviet power: some new word showing the prominent part played by the criminal element, something like 'kakourgocracy' or 'paranomocracy'. Henry George said in *Progress and Poverty* that our civilisation does not require any foreign barbarians for its destruction. It carries in its very bosom the barbarians who will destroy it. Bolshevism consists just in the organisation and gathering of these barbarian forces existing inside contemporary society, hostile to culture and civilisation.

This is a vital point which you miss when you are speaking of Bolshevism in England. You will realise it only when it is too late.

Translated by Paul Leon

Letter V

Ekaterinodar

I shall have to deal with Bolshevism and the history of its development on another occasion. For the present I shall only try to sketch the outlines of the present conditions in Russia and the forces underlying them.

The line of battle of the Volunteer Army of General Denikin against the Bolsheviks, i.e., Soviet Russia, stretches on a long curved front from Odessa to Astrakhan. The central portion of this front, in the direction of Moscow, is holding its own at present, and at the moment of writing the Volunteer Army has conquered Orel and is advancing in the direction of Toula and Briansk. On the sector between Kiev and Odessa fighting is proceeding with the remnant of the Ukrainian Army, i.e., with the Bolsheviks under another name; and the final clearance of this territory from all kinds of Bolsheviks is merely a matter of time. The position of the Volga and the Caucasus is, however, not so good.

The withdrawal of the English forces from Baku and the rest of Transcaucasia – a move so loudly advocated by the English friends of the Bolsheviks – has created many difficulties for the Volunteer Army and given new hope to the Bolsheviks of Baku and Astrakhan. The mountaineers of Dagestan and Circassia revolted at once, and nobody can foresee the end of this new struggle. The Bolsheviks are making desperate attempts to take Tsaritzine and break through to Astrakhan. If they succeed in doing this they will find it easy to join the Dagestan revolt, and then the danger of the spread of Bolshevism over the whole of the Caucasus may become acute. The Bolsheviks will then also succeed in seizing the naphtha districts, which undoubtedly will change their position for the better. The Turkestan and Transcaspian districts are in the full possession of the Bolsheviks.

The position on the Koltchak front seems uncertain. You will certainly have more news than I; and I have already mentioned the possibilities arising from the Bolsheviks reaching the Chinese frontier. Even in the event of Koltchak stopping the Bolshevik advance and Denikin taking Moscow, the Bolsheviks are sure to make their way through the Volga to the Turkestan and the Transcaspian district. Steps are already being taken with this in view. The Turkestan Bolsheviks, so we are told by refugees recently arrived from this district, are busily engaged in spreading propaganda in Central Asia and India. There are centres in Tashkent for training propagandists in all the languages of the East.

The position in Russian areas liberated from the Bolsheviks is by no means easy. Life has been so utterly destroyed that destruction goes on automatically. In Western Russia Jewish pogroms are taking place repeatedly. And we know only too well that this is always connected with previous organisation on the part of the Government. I refer, as an instance, to the well-known book by Prince Ouroussoff, *Notes of a Governor*. In the present case, likewise, the origin of the pogroms is well known. The ghost of the old régime which is still haunting us does not promise anything satisfactory. In the West and East, and in the South and North alike, speculation, profiteering, and the high cost of living are increasing, 'not daily, but hourly', as the expression goes in Russian tales.

The cause of the continuous rise in prices is, besides profiteering, the complete and fantastic inability on the part of the Government to manage its finances.

The direct result of its activities is the loss of popular confidence in paper currency. Different kinds of paper money issued during recent years are repeatedly being 'annulled'. Every time this happens, the immediate result is a new increase in prices and a loss of confidence in other paper currency. Lately, the official at present in charge of finance announced the imminent 'reduction of value' of all kinds of paper currency. Its instant result will undoubtedly be the complete impossibility of buying anything at all.

Obviously we are rapidly approaching a time when life in Russia without profiteering will be impossible. Only by 'barter', i.e., having at any given moment some kind of goods on hand, will it be possible to continue living, as only goods are subjected to an increase in value. To take a simple instance. If you received 1,000 roubles yesterday, these are worth only 500 roubles to-day, and to-morrow perhaps they will be worth 250 roubles. But if you were clever enough to buy some kind of goods you would to-day be worth 2,000 instead of 1,000 roubles. A few days ago such a jump in price happened with sugar. Soft sugar cost 25 roubles (i.e., £2. 10s. at the old rate of exchange) and then it suddenly jumped to 50 roubles. The profits to be made are so obvious that everybody buys or sells something: everybody but the intelligentsia, who have no cash and still live on principles, which have now become ridiculous prejudices.

To the above-named causes of the depreciation in value of the rouble a new one has lately been added. I mean the 'economic war' now carried on by the Republics of the Don, Kouban and Terek against the Volunteer Army.

It would be necessary to resort to history and geography in order to understand the actual meaning of the preceding sentence. I propose simply to describe to you my own position in the midst of all these powers continuously warring against each other. I hope you will gather from it the political aspect of the question.

I am living now at Ekaterinodar. This is the capital of the Kouban region, and is one of the richest towns in Russia in terms of natural wealth. It is situated on the bank of the Kouban River, in the plain of the Northern Caucasus. It has practically no history at all, its reputation being based only on the fevers which rage there. It was founded in the eighteenth century, as can be guessed by its very name, and its appearance bears traces of its origin. The whole town consists merely of streets running into each other at right angles. In short, in normal times it is the most God-forsaken place one can imagine. Hardly anyone of my acquaintance has ever been in Ekaterinodar before. An extensive commerce in grain, oil, and specially tobacco is to be found there, but nothing else. The only noteworthy edifice is a most hideous monument to Catherine II with gnome-like figures of Potemkin and Cossacks round its base. The inhabitants, however, are very proud of this monument; somebody even tried to convince me that it was marvellous. I take it, however, he was being sarcastic. There is a sentry on duty near the monument who does not allow you to touch its gate. If you dare express your opinion aloud you risk your life. The town is more filthy than you can imagine. I do not think there exists a worse smelling spot on earth. When you walk along the brick-paved streets of Ekaterinodar every possible stench of dirt and decomposition meets you. At times you have to walk through a symphony of smells. Nowhere in Europe, Asia, or Africa have I met with such a variety of odours, or ones of such power. I bitterly regret the fact that three years ago I recovered completely from catarrh. What a blessing nasal catarrh would be now!

Another characteristic feature of Ekaterinodar, and one which largely accounts for the preceding one, is the enormous number of dead animals you see in the streets. When leaving your house, you can hardly ever escape tumbling over the body of a dead dog or cat, or a whole family of kittens. A few days ago I was strangely struck by the fact that after half an hour's walk I had not met with any corpse. Hardly had the thought occurred to me than I tumbled over two enormous dead rats, and a few steps further was lying a little black dog on whose carcase thousands of fleas were gathering.

Another time I witnessed a strange scene. It happened on one of the unpaved streets of Ekaterinodar at some distance from the centre. For several days there had been no rain, and in the deep mud, in which the pigs moving on the streets were half submerged, were appearing little dry stands. On one such island, a few steps off the little wooden bridges which here replace the pavement for walkers, were lying two kittens. Near them sat a little girl holding in her arms a big black and white cat, and she was trying to bring the animal's face nearer to the little bodies. The cat obviously disliked it; it looked sad and confused, and obeyed the little girl with apparent reluctance, as sometimes cats do obey little girls. Whilst I was passing, the little girl put her arms round the big cat and looked at me, trying to hide the two little bodies. But when I moved away she again began her play. From the next yard, however, there came such a wave of the very worst odour that I hurried away and never turned back to look if the little girl was still at her play and what it all meant.

At the next corner I met the motor-car of a Kouban Minister. But before I proceed I must explain what this means. Under the old régime, only three years ago, if you ever met a Kouban it was only as a Cossack of the escort. If you have ever been in St Petersburg you are sure to remember these tall, well-built figures in dark blue Circassian dress, with enamelled bullets on the breast, yellow garments and big black lambskin bonnets with red tops (papakha). The Koubans formed the greater part of the very best detachment of Cossacks, who bore the name of His Majesty's Own Escort.

But now the Koubans have become Republicans, and have severed themselves from Russia. They are forming the Kouban Republic, which at present is waging an economic war on the Government of United Russia as represented by the Volunteer Army. The chief characteristic of the Kouban Republic is undoubtedly its flag. It is an unusually harmonious combination of colours – azure, crimson and green; a crimson band in the middle, below and above which are respectively a narrower one of azure, and a like one of green. The Kouban Republic also has a Parliament and Ministers. Every Minister has an official motor-car at his disposal. Such was the motor-car with its azure, crimson and green colours which I met a few minutes after encountering the little girl with the cats.

The Koubans are not the only people who have become Republicans. The Dontzys and Tertzys, formerly of the escort, have also formed their Republics of the Don and Terek. They also possess Ministers of their own, who have Government cars and other privileges. The existence of these Republics is based, firstly, on the very natural desire of their Ministers to keep their cars. (I think that in Western countries one ought to say portfolios, but we know well enough that Western laws are not written for us.) Beyond this, however, the main reason is to be found in the determination of the Cossacks of the Don, Kouban and Terek to preserve the status quo in the matter of land tenure.

The land question in the Cossack regions is very complicated, and promises to provide many riddles and difficulties for the future. The term 'Cossack' is not yet, I think, sufficiently understood by the English reader. Let me state it as clearly as I can. 'Cossack' means – in the regions of the Don, Kouban and Terek – 'the first settlers', as opposed to the later colonists, who are called 'aliens'. During the old régime the Cossacks of each of these regions enjoyed self-determination in military affairs as distinct from the 'aliens'. A feature of their life was the prolonged military service in special Cossack forces. They had to provide their own horses and ammunition. On the other hand, they enjoyed the benefit of large land allotments, very often fifty or sixty acres each. The whole land in these three districts, except a small portion held in private ownership, belonged to the Cossacks, on a communal basis. The aliens, on the contrary, had no rights whatever in the land, enjoyed no allotments, and had to rent their plots from private owners or from the Cossacks.

After the Revolution, which brought about the abolition of all privileges, the land was supposed to be divided equally among the whole population, and the privileges of the Cossacks were naturally to cease. This was the idea of those who owned no land; the Cossacks, however, think otherwise, and have not the smallest desire to give their land up to the aliens. Be it noted that the highlanders of the Kouban and Terek regions, i.e., the actual subjected aborigines, also have a claim on the land. The Cossacks insist on the fact that the land was conquered by their forefathers, and that nobody has the right to expropriate them. Aliens, on the other hand, declare that once the abolition of privileges is an accomplished fact, the land belongs to all. The arguments on both sides are equally strong! What will be the solution of this conflict nobody can predict. Another point is that the 'aliens' are in all three regions in the majority. In the case of a re-allotment being effected, the Cossacks would lose over half of their present possessions. This would be the case if the re-allotments were confined to each separate region. If, however, this measure were to be extended to Russia as a whole, both Cossacks and 'aliens' would be left without land.

But the land question in Russia deserves separate treatment. I will confine myself to the Cossack land. The Cossacks, though in the minority, nevertheless

45

form the government of all three regions; and these governments naturally defend the interests of the 'Cossacks' as against the 'aliens'. The reason for this lies in the fact that the Cossacks were already in possession of some sort of organisation when the Revolution took place, and that the Bolsheviks during the short period of their government based themselves on the 'aliens'. When the Bolsheviks were driven out of the country the government was assumed by the Cossacks. The 'aliens' are considered suspicious; they are not allowed to participate in the government, or, at least, in questions connected with the land problem.

The political organisation of the three regions differs in each of them. The Terek and Don regions are governed solely by a Cossack Assembly, styled the 'Army Council'. The Kouban region, on the other hand, has an Assembly, in the election of which the 'aliens' are allowed to participate. This parliament of the Kouban is furiously democratic in everything but the land question. It chooses to assume a very arrogant attitude towards the government of the Volunteer Army, which it considers reactionary.

You can see from these indications how complicated the problem is. In order to destroy every opportunity of a peaceful settlement of any single question the government of each of these Republics is conducting an economic and tariff war against every other, as I mentioned in my first letter. This war is now being extended to the Volunteer Army, or, as the political leaders say here: it is the Volunteer Army that makes war on them. This situation has been created by different causes, though of a similar character.

The Kouban region, the wealthiest of all in grain and other raw products, objected to all exports which brought back only paper currency of no value. It was prepared to exchange its products solely against other goods. To stop unauthorised exports the Kouban region girdled itself with customs-houses. At every station on this new 'front' trains are stopped for a very long time, all luggage is searched, etc. This has been the rule for six months. But now, since new regions have been liberated from the Bolsheviks, the Don and Terek regions are in the same position. Though these regions have less grain than the Kouban, they still have something. The newly liberated regions have none, or bread is sold there at 40–50 roubles a pound, i.e. ten times the price of bread in the Terek region. Were grain allowed to go, it would at once vanish from the Don and Terek, and be replaced by mountains of paper currency, which the Volunteer Army threatens to 'annul'. There is good reason, it must be admitted, to be distressed.

The Republics decided not to allow any export of grain. The Volunteer Army answered this measure by a declaration that it would not allow any goods to go to the Republics. In other words, the Volunteer Army declared an economic blockade of the unruly Republics; and the Kouban, Terek and Don Governments are confronted with the dilemma of exporting grain, or going without other products: sugar, leather, manufactured goods, etc. The near future will show us how high the prices of bread or other goods will rise. The experience of latter days allows us to predict that we shall have to pay more for both. Such 'conflicts' invariably lead to the benefit of an increased mass of speculators, Armenians, etc.

And all this happens in the neighbourhood nearest to the Bolsheviks, and while the Bolsheviks are still undefeated!

I intended to speak of myself, of my life here. Should I have succeeded in showing you how a day is spent here, you would get a clearer insight into our life. But, as you see, almost every word has to be explained. So far away are we from each other, that one might say we were almost on different planets. Only may there be none of our Bolsheviks on your planet!

Translated by Paul Leon

Epilogue

from *In Denikin's Russia* by C. E. Bechhofer

At last we reached Rostov-on-the-Don (so called to distinguish it from another Rostov near Moscow). I fought my way through the crowded station and took a cab into the town. In a few minutes I was knocking at the door of my friend, Mr Ouspensky. He is a Russian writer who has published one or two books in English also; he is an authority on such subjects as the fourth dimension – if one can be an expert on such intangible things – and has written some entertaining books on India and Indian philosophy. I have had the pleasure of knowing him for some years, in India, England, and pre-Revolutionary Russia. A brilliant series of letters he had sent to the *New Age*, the London weekly, describing conditions in South Russia in the summer and autumn of 1919, made me particularly want to renew his acquaintance. He received me cordially and at once invited me to share his room. I said I would not trouble him, but would go to a hotel. He laughed.

'You cannot get a room in a hotel in Russia to-day,' he said; 'they have all been requisitioned by the Government or by officers.'

'And in private houses?'

'The same thing. Every flat in Rostov has been searched by the billeting officials. They leave one room for each married couple, if these are lucky, and commandeer the rest for officers. I am in this room myself only until to-morrow. The officer who has requisitioned it is a friend of mine, and he has lent it to me for a few days. But he is returning to-morrow, and then we must look out for a new room, if we can find one.'

I looked blank. Were we to spend the next night in the street? Ouspensky smiled at my consternation.

'Don't worry,' he said; 'we shall find a place somewhere. I can see that you are new to the country. For the last two years nobody worries about what will happen to him to-morrow. These are not like the old days when you and I used to meet in Petrograd, and even made appointments two or three days in advance. Never mind, you will soon get used to it. Wait till you have lived under the Bolshevists, as I have! I tell you that until you have experienced Bolshevism, you don't know what the world really contains. Fancy thinking about what will happen to-morrow! What a strange idea!'

Ouspensky showed me his possessions. They consisted of the clothes he was wearing (principally a rather ragged frock-coat, a remnant of former fortunes), a couple of extra shirts and pairs of socks, one blanket, a shabby overcoat, an extra pair of boots, a tin of coffee, a razor, a file and whetstone, and a towel. He assured me that he considered himself exceptionally fortunate to have so much left. On the next day we transferred our belongings to a new dwelling he had discovered for us. This consisted of two small rooms over a kind of barn in the courtyard of a big house. They had been requisitioned by an officer who, having to go up-country on duty for a week or so and being afraid of losing them in the meantime, had lent them to a friend, who in turn hospitably invited Ouspensky and myself to share them with him. In any other place, at any other time, I would have turned up my nose at the rooms. They were small, very cold and draughty, and excessively inconvenient. To get to them one had to ring the porter's bell; he then emerged from his quarters and drove a couple of ferocious dogs into their kennel, after which he would unlock the gate and let us in. When we wanted to go out, we had to go through the same ritual. Sometimes, when the porter was busy or asleep or drunk, one could spend a quarter of an hour outside in the snow, or inside one's door, with a chorus of barking dogs for company. To crown our troubles, the landlord of the house suddenly sent over to tell us to go away, on the ground that we had no right to occupy the barn at all.

In a sense he was right, but we knew exactly what his reason was; he wanted to let the rooms at a fabulous amount to some rich refugee from Bolshevist Russia. We determined to forestall him, and the way we did it will demonstrate fairly clearly how one lives nowadays in Russia. I was sent off in the morning to the Commandant of the Rostov Garrison, General Tarassenkov, who was in charge of all the requisitioning of rooms. I told him that I was an English journalist and in need of a room. Wearily he told me that there were no rooms to be had in Rostov, but he gave me the right to requisition one if I could find it. I told him I thought I knew of a house with some rooms in it, and he promptly sent an officer with me to see. I took him to the house in the garden of which we were staying, and with great dignity the two of us went through the owner's apartments, inquiring who was in each room. All the rooms appeared to be occupied, although I fancied that some of the apparent occupiers were what the Russians call 'dead souls,' i.e. people who no longer existed (the term is taken from Gogol's famous book). However, the officer who was with me turned out to be a friend of the houseowner, and took care not to put awkward questions. In any case, my purpose was served; I was sure that the landlord would no longer dare to order us out of his barn.

And so it proved. During the week or two we spent in Rostov the 'bourjooee' landlord made no further attempt to recover his premises. Our next problem was to get fuel. The rooms were icily cold; draughts blew in every direction; and coal was practically unobtainable in Rostov owing to the breakdown of the transport system. Our host, one Zaharov, got to work to obtain a permit for fuel; soon he returned with a paper that entitled some engineer or other to be given a ton and a half of coal from the Government stores at a greatly reduced price. How Zaharov came into possession of this paper I do not know, and I took care not to inquire. Ouspensky and I went next morning to the treasury of the Don Government to pay in the money. After three hours' waiting in a queue, we were able to pay and get a receipt. This was handed to me, as the least occupied member of the party, to take to the local engineer's office and to obtain a ticket for the coal in exchange for it. It was nearly two o'clock on Saturday afternoon when I reached the office. A clerk kept me waiting for a few minutes until the clock struck; then he looked up and said that I was too late and would have to wait until Monday. I pointed out that I had been waiting some minutes already and proposed that he should give me the ticket I wanted. After some grumbling, he reluctantly opened his book. Then he took my receipt from the Treasury, totted up the total carefully, and announced triumphantly that he could not give me the ticket after all, because I had paid sixty kopecks too little. Now, the whole sum had been some seven hundred roubles, and sixty kopecks were, in any case, only worth a fraction of a penny! I told him that I had waited three hours at the Treasury that morning; he replied, with a smile, that I should have to wait another three hours on Monday to pay in the sixty kopecks! This very characteristic example of Russian officialdom did not impress me as perhaps he expected it to do, and I demanded to see his superior. Oh, impossible; the Chief Engineer never saw anyone without an appointment. So I knocked at the door and walked in. The Chief Engineer was all affability; delighted to meet an Englishman at any time; what could he do for me, and so on. I explained the matter of the sixty kopecks; he roared with laughter, apologised, and called in the official. He then solemnly authorised him to receive the sum of sixty kopecks – approximately one-eighth of a penny – from me, and told him to issue me with the ticket. The official got to work slowly to make out the ticket, but took the opportunity to remark to a lady who was sitting in the office that really the English were becoming unbearable; not only did they receive coal officially, but they actually had the impertinence to come and ask for it privately as well. I begged him not to make incorrect statements about my countrymen and myself in my presence, whereupon he and the lady rebuked me severely for interrupting a private conversation. They said that it was indelicate on my part. This was all part of the task of getting the coal, I thought; so I must be patient. He gave me the ticket at last, but when I offered him a five rouble note (worth about three farthings) in payment, he said that I must give him exactly sixty kopecks, neither more nor less. I said I would call for the change on Monday. Then I hurried off in a cab to the coal dump, which was at the other end of the town. Here I met with a new series of obstructions. No one doubted that the receipt entitled me to the coal, that I had paid for it, and that I was waiting to take it away; but it seemed that the clerk had filled up some part of the ticket not quite correctly, and they suggested that I should come back again on Monday. The prospect of wasting another day on the job, of undertaking another expensive drive out to the suburbs, and, especially, of spending the week-end in a temperature below freezing point, did not appeal to me, and I exerted all my powers to obtain the coal. At last I succeeded in breaking through the red tape – chiefly, I am afraid, on the ground that, as a foreigner, I had been unable to understand all the intricacies of Russian coal control.

I now set off gaily to walk back to Rostov with a ton or so of coal on a cart beside me. The carter assured me privately that he had put on quite a hundredweight more coal than I was entitled to, and asked my permission to load a little on the cart for himself. I made no objection; and he put on two huge lumps. As soon as we got clear of the depot, he stopped the cart in front of a private coal store, carried in the two lumps to the proprietor, and rejoined me with the pleasing news that he had received 200 roubles for them. I reflected that he was doing on a small scale only what very many officials were then doing on a large scale in Russia.

I asked the carter what he thought about things in general, and discovered that he had been conscripted for the Bolshevist army in Kharkov, captured by the Volunteers in the autumn, and by them given the choice of fighting in their armies or of going to work behind the lines. He was not a fighting man, and had gladly chosen the second alternative. I asked him what he thought of the Bolshevists as contrasted with the Volunteers, and he replied that the chief thing to him was that most factories in Bolshevist Russia did not work, whereas those in the anti-Bolshevist parts did, to some extent. Beyond this he did not seem to take much interest in the matter. I asked him who he thought would come out winners. 'Oh,' he said, 'the Bolshevists, for sure. You see, they have warm clothes.'

I arrived home in triumph with my ton of coal, much to the admiration of myself and my friends. For once, sheer aplomb had broken through the meshes of Russian official procedure, and we had got in one day what might have taken a month or two with less aggressive methods. In high glee, we called in the man who attended to the fires of the whole household. He was a taciturn man from Moscow, grimy with coal dust. Accustomed to deal with wood fires, this coal fuel was rather beyond his powers, and we soon had occasion to notice that he was more skilful in extinguishing the fire than in keeping it alight. In fact, we began to get frightened whenever he came to look at it. A few glasses of home-made vodka – a drink unobtainable in shops, by General Denikin's orders – soon thawed him, and I was able to draw him out a little. He had come down south, he said, to get out of Bolshevist Moscow, because 'you can't get anything to eat there.' A lot of factory workers, he said, especially those who had returned from prisoners' camps in Germany, had made demonstrations against the Bolshevists, but in the factory where he had been working the ringleaders had been arrested by a special detachment of the Red Guard, led away, and never seen again. Every 'more sensible' person, he said, was opposed to the Bolshevists, but the young firebrands were with them. 'But,' he added, 'if only the Volunteers had got as near to Moscow as Tula, all Moscow would have risen and cast off the Bolshevists.' He was irritated at the thought of the Bolshevists advancing on Rostov. 'It means we shan't have anything to eat again!'

The fire had a wonderful effect upon our spirits. Living as one did in Russia, from hour to hour, a good fire was a thing to make a fuss about. We had found a quantity of spirit in one of the cupboards in the room, and, despite Zaharov's protests, Ouspensky proceeded to transform it into vodka with the addition of some orange peel. He told Zaharov that the real owner would never get back to Rostov in time to use it before the Bolshevists came – a prophecy which proved to be accurate – and that, if we did not drink it, the Commissars would. Se we began to drink it.

'People have been drinking since the beginning of the world,' remarked Ouspensky suddenly; 'but they have never found anything to go better with vodka than a salted cucumber.'

With which remark he entered upon a series of reminiscences of his life in Moscow in the happy days before the War, which sounded queerly when one contrasted them with the misery and privations he and every one else was now enduring. There was nothing of the reactionary in Ouspensky's praise of the good old days; his sister had died in prison as a political offender, and he himself had been no stranger to the revolutionary movement. One has to visit Russia, stay there a while and spend one's time with Russians, to understand what the last six years have meant to them. But I am interrupting Ouspensky.

'It was when I was a young man in Moscow,' he was saying, 'and my cousin once gave a party. We brewed the vodka together. It was a marvellous brew. There was one man there, the sort of type one sees only in Russia; a young man with long hair, a long beard, long moustaches, and a sad, far-away look in his eyes. Well, after he had one glass of our vodka, he got straight up from his chair and walked out of the house and into the nearest hairdresser's. There he made them run the clippers all over his head, and shave him, and he came out as bare of hair as an egg, and went straight home to bed. That shows you what good vodka can do!

'By the way,' he said, 'did you ever hear of the Chief of Police here in Rostov just after the outbreak of the Revolution. One of his clerks found him in his office, examining some documents very carefully. At last he looked up and said, scratching his head, "Ye—es, I can understand that the proletariat of the world ought to unite; but what I can't understand is why they should want to unite at Rostov-on-the-Don." '

'To-night,' remarked Zaharov with equal gravity, 'we shall have hot water. We shall be able to wash our faces, clean our teeth, and indulge in all sorts of similar unaccustomed amusements.'

'Don't interrupt me,' said Ouspensky. 'I was remarking that every policeman in Moscow in the old days knew me by my Christian name, because, unlike most people, when I was drunk, I always tried to compose quarrels and not to start them. Besides, I used to give them big tips. And all the porters at the restaurants used to know me, and when there was a row on, they used to telephone to me to come round and stop it. One night I remember I got home with the left sleeve of my overcoat missing. How I lost it, and where, I have never discovered, although I have given the matter very careful thought. Indeed, I once thought of writing a book about it.'

'Well,' said I, 'where shall we be in a month's time, I wonder?'

They both turned on me. 'It's clear,' they said, 'you've never lived under the Bolshevists. If you had, you wouldn't ask that sort of question. You would acquire the sort of psychology that does not admit reflections of that kind.'

'And yet,' said Ouspensky, 'when I was under the Bolsheviks last year, I did once consider the future. I was at Essentuki, in the North Caucasus. The Bolsheviks had requisitioned all the books in the place and taken them into the school there. I went to the Commissar and asked him to make me librarian. I had been schoolmaster there previously. You didn't know I had been a schoolmaster since the Revolution, did you? [He turned to me.] Yes, and I've been a house-porter, too. Well, the Commissar didn't quite know what a librarian was, but I explained to him. He was a simple man and began to be almost frightened of me when I told him that I had written books of my own. So he made me librarian and I put up a big notice on the door saying that this was the "ESSENTUKI SOVIET LIBRARY." My idea was to keep the books safe, without mixing them up, so that when the Bolsheviks went away, they could be given back to their owners. I arranged them nicely, and spent my time reading some of them. Then one night the Cossacks came and drove the Bolsheviks out. I ran round to the school in spite of the firing and tore down the word "Soviet", for fear the Cossacks came and destroyed everything, and so it read simply "ESSENTUKI LIBRARY." And next day I started to hand the books back to their owners. Not a soul had been to the library all the time, so no harm was done in breaking it up.'

'Still,' said Zaharov, 'Bechhofer's question has a certain theoretical interest. I wonder where we shall be in a month's time.'

'You may wonder as much as you like,' said Ouspensky; 'but you will never find better vodka than this.'

A month later I wrote the following entry in my diary:

'I can answer my own question now. I am at Novorossisk, writing this. Ouspensky is, I believe, at Ekaterinodar, trying to get his wife away to the comparative safety of the seashore. I do not know if I shall ever see him again, or where. Zaharov died three days ago of small-pox, contracted at Rostov at the very time when we were living with him. And the Bolsheviks are at Rostov.'